ALASKAN IDITAROD ADVENTURE

Represent and Solve Problems Involving Multiplication

Wendy Strout

Rosen Readers

Rosen Classroom™

New York

Published in 2015 by The Rosen Publishing Group, Inc.
29 East 21st Street, New York, NY 10010

Book Design: Mickey Harmon

Photo Credits: Cover, pp. 5 (main), 13, 15 Anchorage Daily News/Contributor/McClatchy-Tribune/Getty Images; pp. 3, 4, 6, 8, 10, 12, 14, 16, 18, 20, 22–24 (background) cluckva/Shutterstock.com; p. 5 (inset) AridOcean/Shutterstock.com; p. 6 http://en.wikipedia.org/wiki/File:Iditarod_Trail_Seward_500.jpg; p. 7 Dennis Macdonald/Photolibrary/Getty Images; p. 9 Matt Cooper/Shutterstock.com; p. 11 Mark Thiessen/AP Images; p. 16 mariait/Shutterstock.com; p. 17 Marcel Jancovic/Shutterstock.com; p. 19 Andrey_Kuzmin/Shutterstock.com; p. 21 Peggy Fagerstrom/AP Images; p. 22 Dmitry Kalinovsky/Shutterstock.com.

Library of Congress Cataloging-in-Publication Data

Strout, Wendy, author.
Alaskan Iditarod adventure : represent and solve problems involving multiplication / Wendy Strout.
pages cm. — (Math masters. Operations and algebraic thinking)
Includes index.
ISBN 978-1-4777-4962-3 (pbk.)
ISBN 978-1-4777-4963-0 (6-pack)
ISBN 978-1-4777-6411-4 (library binding)
1. Iditarod (Race)—Juvenile literature. 2. Multiplication—Juvenile literature. 3. Iditarod National Historic Trail (Alaska)—Juvenile literature. I. Title.
SF440.15.S77 2015
513.2'13—dc23
2014001688

Manufactured in the United States of America

CPSIA Compliance Information: Batch #WS15RC: For further information contact Rosen Publishing, New York, New York at 1-800-237-9932.

CONTENTS

DOGSLED DREAMS

Many different kinds of races take place around the world—from footraces to car races. One **unique** kind of race is a dogsled race. In a dogsled race, teams of dogs pull sleds through the snow.

I live in Alaska, which is the home of the most famous dogsled race in the world–the Iditarod. When I grow up, I want to be a musher, or dogsled driver, in the Iditarod.

The Iditarod takes place every year around the beginning of March. It follows a trail from Anchorage to Nome. That's a **distance** of around 1,150 miles (1,851 km).

ALASKA
NOME
CANADA
ANCHORAGE

CREATING THE IDITAROD

Joe Redington Sr. was a musher who played a large role in the creation of the Iditarod. He helped create a shorter dogsled race in 1967 to celebrate the 100th anniversary of Alaska becoming a U.S. territory.

Redington helped prepare 9 miles (14 km) of the Iditarod National Historical Trail for the race. To prepare 9 miles, he could have worked on 3 miles each day for 3 days.

I know that 3 times 3 equals 9.

$3 \times 3 = 9$

After races in 1967 and 1969, people lost interest in the idea of a race across the Iditarod Trail. However, Redington continued to work hard to make it a reality. In 1973, the first Iditarod race from Anchorage to Nome took place. The winner was Dick Wilmarth. He took nearly 3 weeks to finish the race.

I know there are 7 days in each week. Using multiplication, I can find out how many days are in 3 weeks.

In this equation, or math problem, I can use a question mark to stand for the missing number of days in 3 weeks. After I multiply 7 by 3, I see that the answer is 21 days.

$$7 \times 3 = ?$$

$$7 \times 3 = 21$$

FINISHING THE RACE

In 1973, 22 mushers crossed the Iditarod finish line. The race has grown a lot since that year. Over 400 mushers have finished the Iditarod since it began. They've come from over 20 different U.S. states as well as many different countries. I hope to be a part of that group of Iditarod finishers someday!

The record for the most mushers to finish an Iditarod was set in 2004, when 77 mushers finished.

If the 77 Iditarod finishers were broken into equal groups of 7 mushers, how many groups would there need to be? I can use multiplication to find the answer. What number makes 77 when multiplied by 7? The answer is 11.

$$77 = ? \times 7$$

$$77 = 11 \times 7$$

THE NORTHERN AND SOUTHERN TRAILS

The Iditarod National Historical Trail has 2 **sections**: a northern trail and a southern trail. During the early years of the race, only the northern trail was used. Now, the northern trail is used in even years, and the southern trail is used in odd years.

Each trail has a **series** of checkpoints, or places to stop and rest, in towns and villages between Anchorage and Nome. The northern trail has 26 checkpoints. What number, when multiplied by 2, gives you 26?

I know that 13 multiplied by 2 equals 26. Knowing basic multiplication facts makes it easy to find missing numbers in equations.

? x 2 = 26

13 x 2 = 26

I live in Grayling, which is a town along the southern trail of the Iditarod. The southern trail also passes through the town of Iditarod. It's now a ghost town. This means no one lives there anymore, and most of the buildings that used to be there are no longer standing.

The southern trail has 27 checkpoints. If there were 9 groups of checkpoints, how many checkpoints would be in each group?

I use multiplication to find the missing number of checkpoints in each group. I find what number makes 27 when multiplied by 9.

$$27 = 9 \times ?$$

$$27 = 9 \times 3$$

SPECIAL SLED DOGS

My dogs, Lucky and Ace, are Alaskan huskies. The Alaskan husky is a very popular kind of sled dog. These dogs are often used to pull sleds in the Iditarod because they're very strong and fast. They're also able to handle the very **harsh** winter conditions in Alaska.

Most teams in the Iditarod have 16 dogs. What number, when multiplied by 4, equals 16? I use division to find the answer, which is 4.

HUSKY

Multiplication and division are closely related. I can find the missing number in a multiplication equation by setting up a simple division equation. If 16 ÷ 4 = 4, then I know 4 x 4 = 16.

$4 \times ? = 16$

$16 \div 4 = 4$

$4 \times 4 = 16$

Sometimes it's hard for me to keep track of 2 dogs. I can't imagine keeping track of all the dogs that race in the Iditarod every year! Each dog in the race is given a microchip. This is a small computer chip put under the dog's skin. The chip is so small it doesn't hurt the dog. It helps track where the dog is.

Each chip has its own code number with 8 **digits**. How many total digits would there be for 10 dogs?

The microchip is usually put on the back of a dog's neck or behind its ear. **Collar** tags are also used to keep track of the dogs.

$8 \times 10 = ?$

THE WIDOW'S LAMP

When sled dogs carried goods and mail across Alaska long ago, a lamp was lit outside of a roadhouse along the trail. This told everyone that a musher and a team of dogs were on the trail. The fire in the lamp wasn't put out until the team got there safely.

Today, the "Widow's Lamp" is lit in Nome when the Iditarod begins in Anchorage. The fire isn't put out until the last team crosses the finish line.

If there were 36 roadhouses on the trail that were broken into 4 equal groups, how many roadhouses were in each group?

36 = 4 x ?

MY OWN IDITAROD ADVENTURE

The Iditarod is the most famous race of its kind, but it's not the only one. There are at least a dozen other major dogsled races in Alaska every winter. My home state is the most popular place in the world for dogsled racing.

Being a musher in the Iditarod isn't easy. The conditions for both people and dogs are very harsh. However, I still hope to be an Iditarod musher someday!

It takes years of training to be an Iditarod musher.

GLOSSARY

collar (KAH-luhr) A band, strip, or chain worn around the neck.

digit (DIH-juht) Any of the numerals from 1 to 9 and usually the symbol 0.

distance (DIHS-tuhns) The space between two points.

harsh (HARSH) Causing discomfort or pain.

section (SEHK-shun) A part cut off or separated.

series (SIHR-eez) A number of things arranged in order and connected by being alike in some way.

unique (yoo-NEEK) Special or different from anything else.

INDEX

Due to the changing nature of Internet links, The Rosen Publishing Group, Inc., has developed an online list of websites related to the subject of this book. This site is updated regularly. Please use this link to access the list: **www.powerkidslinks.com/mm/oat/aia**